ANIMALS AT RISK

AFRICAN ELEPHANTS AT RISK

SAVING THESE MAJESTIC MAMMALS

BY KATHRYN CLAY

CAPSTONE PRESS
a capstone imprint

Published by Capstone Press, an imprint of Capstone
1710 Roe Crest Drive, North Mankato, Minnesota 56003
capstonepub.com

Copyright © 2026 by Capstone. All rights reserved. No part of this publication may be reproduced in whole or in part, or stored in a retrieval system, or transmitted in any form or by any means, electronic, mechanical, photocopying, recording, or otherwise, without written permission of the publisher.

Library of Congress Cataloging-in-Publication Data is available on the Library of Congress website

ISBN: 9798875221712 (hardcover)
ISBN: 9798875221668 (paperback)
ISBN: 9798875221675 (ebook PDF)

Summary: African elephants may seem stronger than anything around them, but they are at risk of dying out. Readers will learn what is causing these creatures to be endangered, including climate change, shrinking habitats, and human hunters, as well as what people can do to help.

Editorial Credits
Editor: Ashley Kuehl; Designer: Elijah Blue; Media Researcher: Jo Miller; Production Specialist: Tori Abraham

Image Credits
Alamy: Imago, 20, Mark Kerrison, 25; Associated Press: Kin Cheung, 22; Getty Images: Andrew Wasike/Anadolu Agency, 21, iStock/monkeybusinessimages, 28, iStock/Smaks K, 17, Martin Harvey, 15, Michael D. Kock, 19; Shutterstock: Alese Watson, 23, David Rajter, 13 (middle), DeawSS, 4 (heart icon), fokke baarssen, 7, hansen.matthew.d, 29, Henk Bogaard, 9, 14, imranhridoy, 4 (trees icon), iulianbugasa, 27, KensCanning, 13 (bottom), Moch. Firman Ardiansyah, throughout (elephant head icon), muratart, 5, Nancy Pauwels, 11 (bottom), nexusby, 4 (temperature icon), Piu_Piu, 26, Roger de la Harpe, 11 (top), Stefan Balaz, 4 (arrow icon), Viktor Tanasiichuk, 11 (map), Villiers Steyn, 6, Volodymyr Burdiak, cover

Design Elements
Shutterstock: Pixels Park, Textures and backgrounds

Any additional websites and resources referenced in this book are not maintained, authorized, or sponsored by Capstone. All product and company names are trademarks™ or registered® trademarks of their respective holders.

Printed and bound in China. 006276

TABLE OF CONTENTS

CHAPTER 1
A DAY IN THE LIFE......................................5

CHAPTER 2
GET TO KNOW THE
AFRICAN ELEPHANT 10

CHAPTER 3
ENDANGERED STATUS............................18

CHAPTER 4
WHAT CAN PEOPLE DO TO HELP?........24

GLOSSARY 30
READ MORE 31
INTERNET SITES 31
INDEX 32
ABOUT THE AUTHOR.......32

Words in **bold** are in the glossary.

WHAT MAKES AN ANIMAL ENDANGERED?

NUMBER OF ANIMALS:
VERY LOW OR SHRINKING FAST

HABITAT LOSS:
BIG DECREASE IN NATURAL HABITAT

RANGE REDUCTION:
SHRINKING AREA WHERE IT CAN LIVE

BREEDING DECLINE:
FEWER ANIMALS HAVING YOUNG

THREATS:
HIGH RISK OF POACHING, DISEASE, OR CLIMATE CHANGE

CHAPTER 1
A DAY IN THE LIFE

An African elephant grazes under the warm sun. Its big ears flap gently, keeping it cool. Nearby, a baby elephant explores its new world. The herd moves slowly through the tall grass before stopping at a watering hole. The elephant dips its trunk into the water. Birds perch on its back, picking off insects. The loud calls between elephants can be heard for miles, letting everyone know where they are.

DAILY LIFE

African elephants spend their days eating, drinking, and taking baths to stay clean and cool. They use their trunks to grab food and water. The trunks act like hoses to spray water over their warm bodies.

Elephants use their trunks in some of the same ways humans use hands. They can pick up water and put it in their mouths.

Traveling as a group protects elephants from danger.

Elephants talk to each other using gentle touches and sounds such as trumpets and rumbles. They travel in groups called herds. Elephants in a herd look after one another. They make sure everyone is safe. Few animals are as social as elephants. They work together to care for the whole group and create strong family connections.

ENDANGERED

It might seem that such big animals would be safe from harm. But African elephants can't protect themselves from all dangers. **Poaching**, habitat loss, and conflicts with people are causing their numbers to go down.

It is illegal to kill elephants. But poachers still kill elephants for their tusks, which sell for a lot of money. People build homes and farms where elephants once lived. Elephants sometimes eat the crops on these farms. Farmers may hurt them to protect their crops. All of these problems are making it hard for elephants to survive.

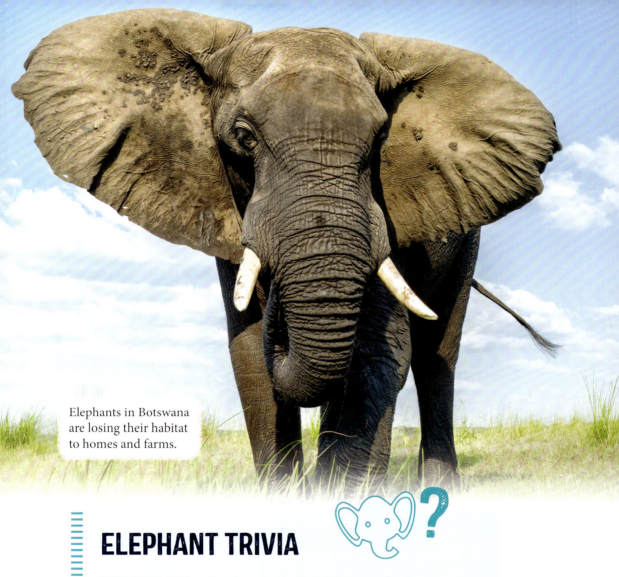

Elephants in Botswana are losing their habitat to homes and farms.

ELEPHANT TRIVIA

QUESTION: What body part helps African elephants keep cool in their hot environments?

ANSWER: African elephants have large ears. They flap their ears to lower their body temperature and keep cool.

— CHAPTER 2 —
GET TO KNOW THE AFRICAN ELEPHANT

African elephants live in many places across Africa, including the Kenyan plains and Tanzanian forests. These big areas have lots of space where the elephants can find food.

Two kinds of elephants live in Africa. They look a lot alike, except for their size. **Savanna** elephants are larger. They live in open areas with few trees. The open spaces allow them more room to grow. Their larger size keeps them safe from predators. Forest elephants live in **rainforests**. They are smaller than savanna elephants. Their small size makes it easy to move through the thick trees and shrubs of their habitat.

ASIAN ELEPHANTS

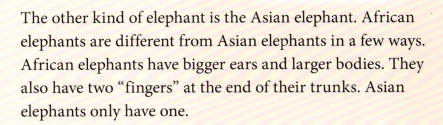

The other kind of elephant is the Asian elephant. African elephants are different from Asian elephants in a few ways. African elephants have bigger ears and larger bodies. They also have two "fingers" at the end of their trunks. Asian elephants only have one.

LIFE CYCLE

Elephants in the wild can live to be 60 to 70 years old. Older elephants show younger ones where to find food and water.

Female elephants and young male elephants live in family groups called herds. An older female called a matriarch leads the group. A herd includes her daughters and their calves.

When males are about 13 years old, they leave their mother's herd. Then they live alone or join other male elephants. Males return to the herd to **mate** with females.

TUSKS

All African elephants have tusks. Female Asian elephants do not. And only some male Asian elephants have them.

AFRICAN ELEPHANT
OR
ASIAN ELEPHANT?

Can you tell an African elephant from an Asian elephant? Find the differences between the elephants in these pictures.

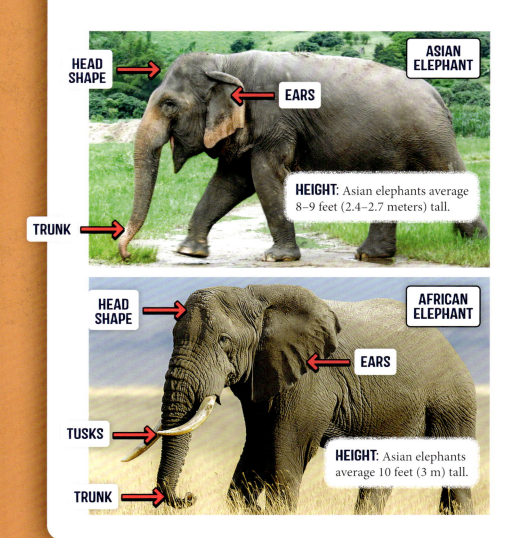

13

WEAPONS AND DEFENSES

An African elephant's size may be its best defense. They are the largest land animals in the world. An adult male can grow up to 13 feet (4 m) tall. It can weigh 14,000 pounds (6,350 kilograms). That's as heavy as two cars!

Tusks are long teeth that stick out from an elephant's mouth. Both males and females have tusks. Forest elephant tusks are straight. Savanna elephant tusks are curved. They use them to dig for water, strip bark from trees to eat, and defend themselves against predators.

An elephant's skin is thick. The tough skin protects them from thorns, bites, and the sun.

ELEPHANT TRIVIA

QUESTION: How big is a baby elephant?

ANSWER: Baby elephants weigh about 200 pounds (90 kg) at birth.

FOOD AND FOOD SOURCES

Elephants need to eat a lot. They spend most of their day searching for food and eating. Elephants are **herbivores**. They eat grass, leaves, fruit, and bark. They use their long trunks to grab food from trees and the ground.

The savanna has rain for six to eight months. That's followed by a dry season. During the dry season, elephants travel to rivers and other water sources. They **migrate** long distances to find food and water.

ELEPHANT TRIVIA

QUESTION: How much does an African elephant eat each day?

ANSWER: An adult elephant can eat about 300 pounds (136 kg) of food daily.

CHAPTER 3
ENDANGERED STATUS

African elephants are disappearing. More of them are dying than are being born. If an animal is **endangered**, very few of them are left. They are at risk of becoming extinct, or disappearing completely. Hunting, habitat destruction, or other threats can make species go extinct.

Millions of elephants roamed throughout Africa in the 1900s. Now, fewer than 500,000 remain in the wild.

Far fewer elephants roam the grasslands of Africa than in the past.

Conservation efforts protect African elephants and help their populations grow. These efforts include anti-poaching laws and habitat restoration. Educating people about the importance of elephants can also help.

ENVIRONMENTAL RISKS

Environmental risks affecting African elephants include **droughts**, wildfires, and diseases. In a drought, there is very little rain. Water sources dry up. Without enough water, elephants can become weak. Their stressed bodies are more likely to catch diseases. These diseases can pass quickly between elephants, killing entire herds. Climate change is causing droughts to happen more often than they used to.

Elephants search for food and water in drought-affected areas.

Droughts also increase the risk of wildfires. Wildfires can destroy large areas of land. Trees and grass burn. Elephants lose these plants as a source of food.

ELEPHANT TRIVIA

QUESTION: How does elephant poop help the land?

ANSWER: Elephant poop spreads seeds. Those seeds can grow into plants in new places.

RISKS CREATED BY HUMANS

Humans are the biggest threat to elephant populations. More than 100,000 elephants have been hunted illegally in the last 10 years. Poachers hunt African elephants for their ivory tusks. Ivory was once a symbol of wealth. It was carved into jewelry and statues. Piano keys and chess pieces were made of it. Most countries have laws against selling ivory. But some people still pay a lot of money for it.

Hong Kong police took these elephant tusks from people who were bringing them into the country illegally. These tusks were valued at $1.5 million.

People also build homes and farms in areas where elephants live. When that happens, elephants lose their homes. They struggle to find enough food. Sometimes they wander onto farms and destroy crops. Farmers sometimes hurt or kill elephants to protect their land.

CHAPTER 4
WHAT CAN PEOPLE DO TO HELP?

Many people are trying to protect African elephants. The International Elephant Federation works to reduce conflicts between elephants and people. They also create protected areas where elephants can live safely. Animals in a **sanctuary** are protected by guards. The guards work to keep poachers away. They search for elephant traps and destroy them. These efforts help to create safe places for elephants to live and grow.

GROUPS WORKING TO HELP AFRICAN ELEPHANTS

World Wildlife Fund (WWF): Educates and partners with local communities

Elephant Crisis Fund: Raises money for projects working to save elephants

Save the Elephants: Researches the science of elephants

African Wildlife Foundation: Protects elephant habitats

Kids can also be part of the effort to save African elephants. Telling friends and family about the problems elephants face is a good start. Everyone can learn about and avoid products made from ivory.

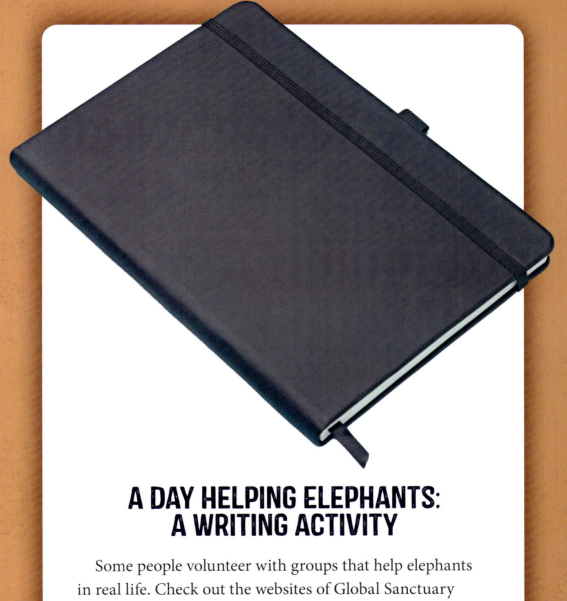

A DAY HELPING ELEPHANTS: A WRITING ACTIVITY

Some people volunteer with groups that help elephants in real life. Check out the websites of Global Sanctuary for Elephants or Kindred Spirit Elephant Sanctuary. Imagine you spend a few days working with one of these groups. Write a journal entry describing what you did and saw. Write about your experiences and your important role in keeping these animals safe.

Another way to help is by adopting an elephant. Special programs support their care. Some people organize fundraisers, such as bake sales or car washes. They give the money to groups that protect elephants.

Everybody's voice has power. Kids and adults can write letters to lawmakers. We can ask them to support laws that protect elephants and their habitats.

It's up to all of us to work together to protect these incredible creatures. By supporting efforts to stop poaching, conserve their habitats, and educate others, we can keep these majestic animals roaming the African plains and forests.

GLOSSARY

conservation (khan-sur-VAY-shun)—the protection of animals and plants

drought (DROUT)—a long period of weather with little or no rainfall

endangered (en-DANE-jurd)—at risk of dying out

herbivore (HUR-buh-vor)—an animal that eats only plants

mate (MAYT)—to join together to produce young

migrate (MYE-grate)—to travel from one place to another

poaching (POCHE-ing)—illegal hunting

rainforest (RAYN-for-ist)—a thick forest where rain falls almost every day

sanctuary (SANGK-choo-er-ee)—a place where animals are cared for and protected

savanna (suh-VAN-uh)—a flat, grassy area with few or no trees

READ MORE

Animal Reads. *All Things Elephants for Kids*. Berlin, Germany: Admore Publishing, 2022.

Nargi, Lela. *Elephants on the Move: A Day with an Asian Elephant Family*. North Mankato, MN: Capstone Editions, 2023.

Orr, Tamra B. *Awesome Animals of Africa*. Mount Joy, PA: Curious Fox Books, 2024.

INTERNET SITES

African Elephant
kids.nationalgeographic.com/animals/mammals/facts/african-elephant

African Elephant
sdzwildlifeexplorers.org/animals/african-elephant

African Elephant Facts
worldwildlife.org/species/african-elephant

INDEX

Asian elephants, 11, 12, 13

babies, 4, 5, 12, 15

climate change, 4, 20
communication, 5, 7
conservation, 19, 24, 25, 26, 27, 28, 29

diseases, 20

ears, 5, 9, 11, 13
eating, 5, 6, 8, 10, 12, 15, 16, 17, 20, 21, 23

habitats, 4, 8, 9, 10, 16, 18, 19, 23, 25, 28, 29
herds, 5, 7, 12, 20

life cycle, 12

mating, 12
migration, 16

poaching, 4, 8, 18, 19, 22, 24, 29
predators, 10, 15

sanctuaries, 24
size, 8, 10, 11, 13, 14, 15
skin, 15

trunks, 5, 6, 11, 13, 16
tusks, 8, 12, 13, 15, 22

ABOUT THE AUTHOR

Kathryn Clay has written more than 100 nonfiction books for kids. Her books cover a wide range of topics, including everything from sign language to space travel. When she's not writing, Kathryn works at a college, helping students develop their critical thinking and study skills. She holds master's degrees in literature and creative writing from Minnesota State University, Mankato.

Kathryn lives in southern Minnesota with her family and an energetic goldendoodle. Together, they make sustainable, eco-friendly choices whenever possible.